Author
Marcos Habif

New Edition
Edited by
F. Dennis Renick
2020

HOW TO PLAY KEYBOARDS FOR KIDS
Kids Book 4

How to play the
PIANO
.....instantly

ABSOLUTE
BEGINNERS

How to play the

PIANO

.....instantly

For Beginners

**Design / Production
Wm Osborne**

Introducing, Special Assistant; 'Half-note'

*This book series is intended to show anyone
how to quickly play literally thousands of songs
with no previous musical instrument experience.
It is not intended to make you sound like a professional, but to quickly and easily enjoy making music
on your own.
We recommend that the first reading of this book
be done while viewing the video[available separately]
in order to follow along.*

Danny Dog Says
"Remember Practice makes
perfect! If you want to be
successful as in life you must
apply yourself. Some
things seem hard but after
you continue dedicating
time to them you will
find they become easier.
So don't give up on your
goals!"

Page 3

Fig. A The Left Hand

The Fingers on the left hand are numbered from the thumb to the pinkie, #1 - 5.

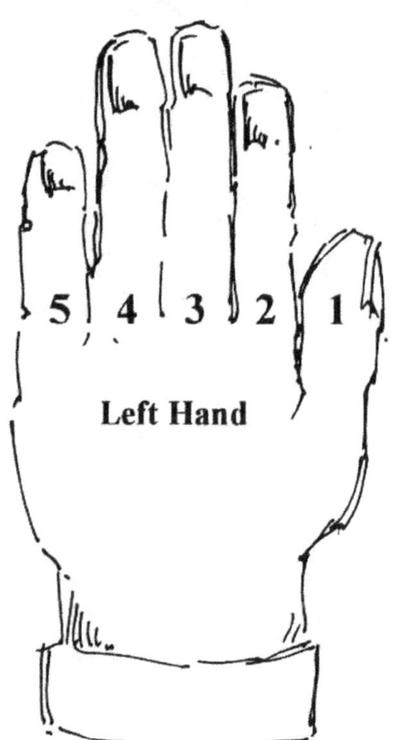

Fig. B Middle 'C'

'C' is the note on the keyboard just before any group of two black notes.

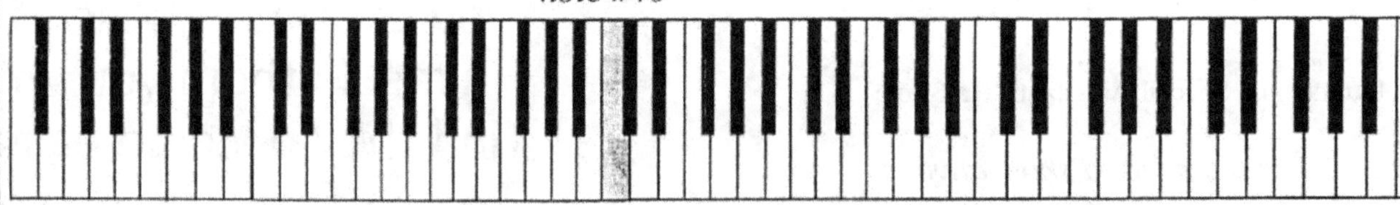

The middle 'C', as it sounds, is about in the middle of the keyboard. If you count every note starting with the bottom note of the keyboard (on your left), the middle 'C' is the 40th note.

Clarence

Fig. C

The numbers on the keys represent the finger numbers for the left hand. Place your fingers on each of these keys at the same time -- this is the position your left hand will be in, making it easy to reach any of these notes.

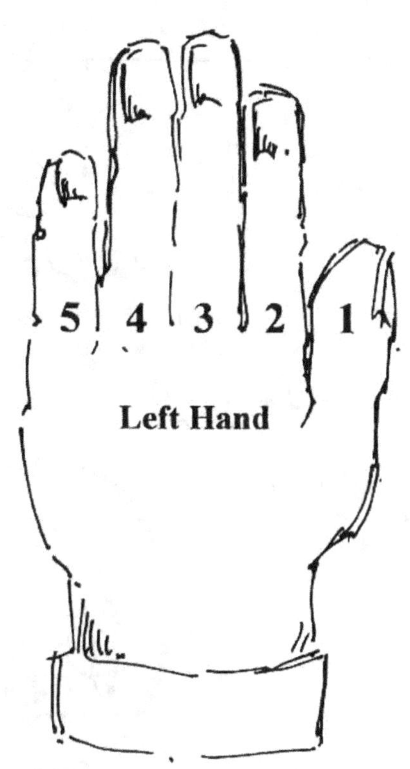

Davey

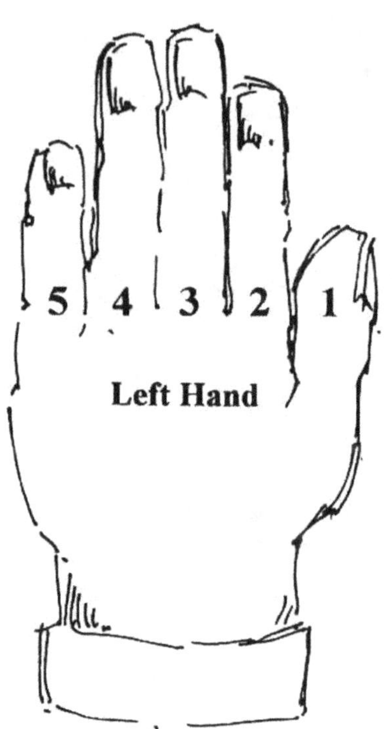

Fig. D Clementine (*left hand*)

$\frac{3}{4}$ c / / | c / / |

c / / | g / / |

g / / | c / / |

g / / | c ‖

Eddie

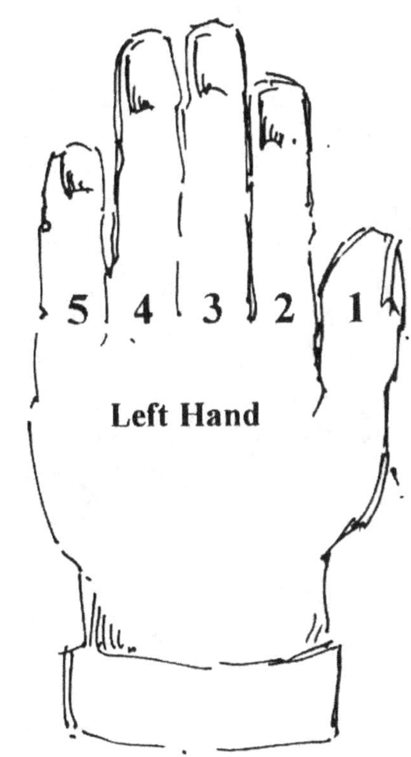

$$\frac{4}{4} c \ / \quad | \ c \quad g \ |$$

$$g \ / \quad | \ g \quad c \ |$$

$$c \ / \quad | \ c \quad g \ |$$

$$g \ / \quad | \ c \ / \ \|$$

Frankie

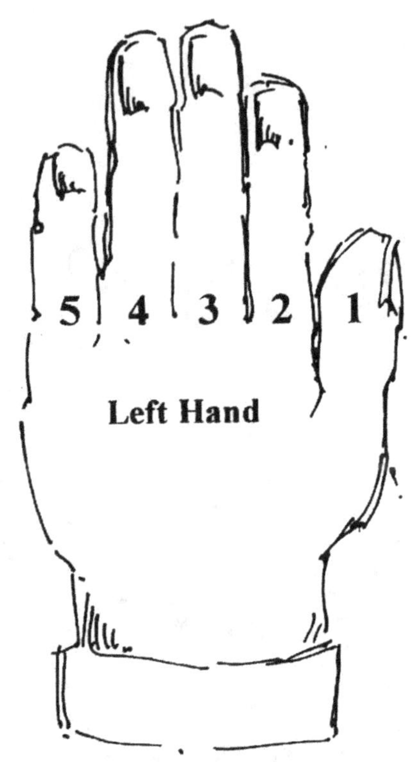

Fig. F Row, Row, Your Boat

$\frac{4}{4}$ c / | c / |

c / | g c |

c / | c / |

c / | g c ||

George

Fig.G Mary Had a Little Lamb

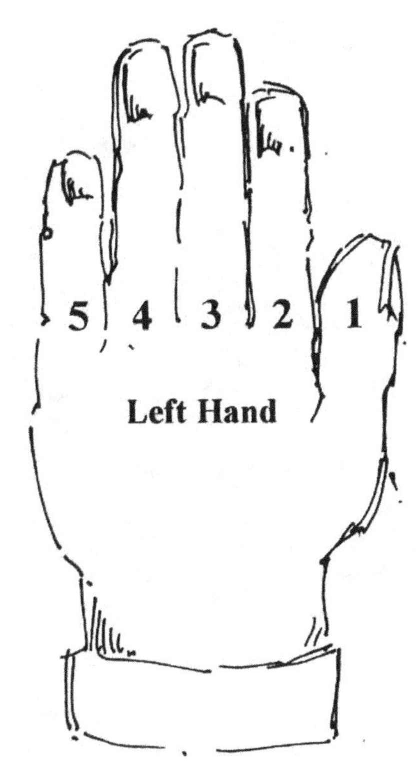

$$\frac{4}{4}\ \text{c} / \quad | \ \text{g} \quad \text{c} \ |$$

$$\text{c} / \quad | \ \text{g} \quad \text{c} \ |$$

(2nd verse) $\text{c} / \quad | \ \text{g} \quad \text{c} \ |$

$$\text{c} / \quad | \ \text{g} \quad \text{c} \ ||$$

Alice

Fig. H The Right Hand

The fingers on the right hand are numbered just like the left hand, from the thumb to the pinki.

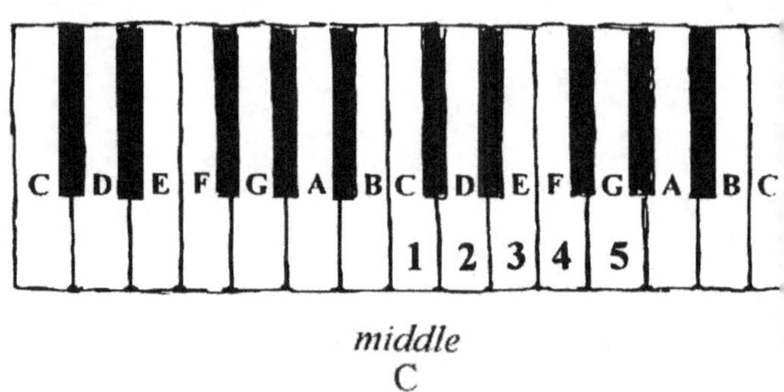

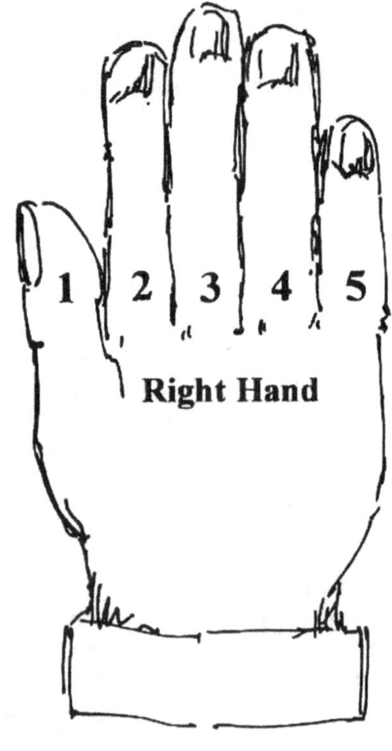

The
Do-Re-Me
Gang
Clarence
DO
George
SOL
Davey
RE
Alice
LA
Eddie
ME
Bobby
Half-note
TI
Frankie
FA
Carol
DO

Bobby and Half-note

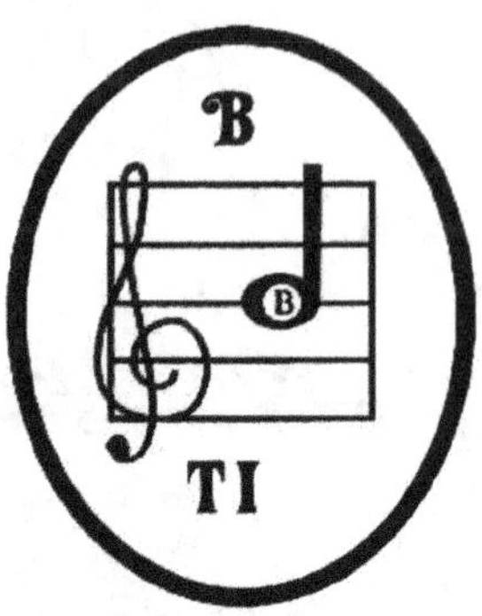

Fig.I The Rest of 'C' Chord

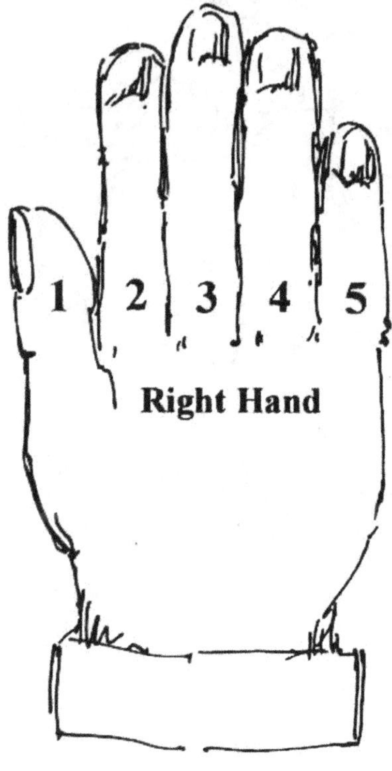

Clementine

$\frac{3}{4}$ c / / | c / / |

c / / | g / / |

g / / | c / / |

g / / | c ||

Carol

Fig.J The 'G' Chord (right hand)

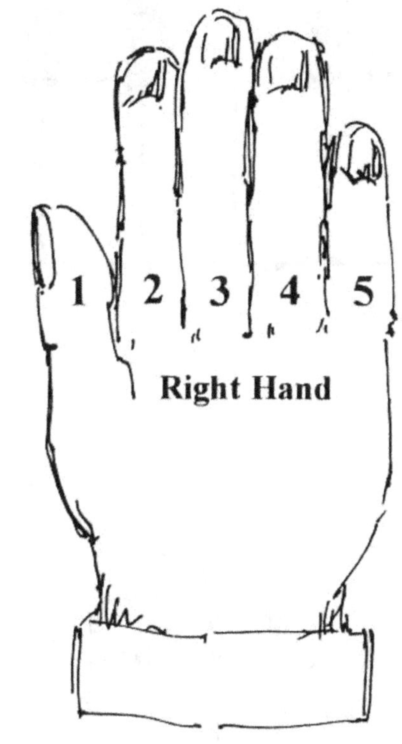

Tom Dooley

$$\frac{4}{4}\ \text{c}\ /\quad |\ \text{c}\quad \text{g}^7\ |$$

$$\text{g}^7\quad |\ \text{g}^7\quad \text{c}\ |$$

$$\text{c}\ /\quad |\ \text{c}\quad \text{g}^7\ |$$

$$\text{g}^7\quad |\ \text{c}\ /\quad \|$$

Fig. K Both Hands

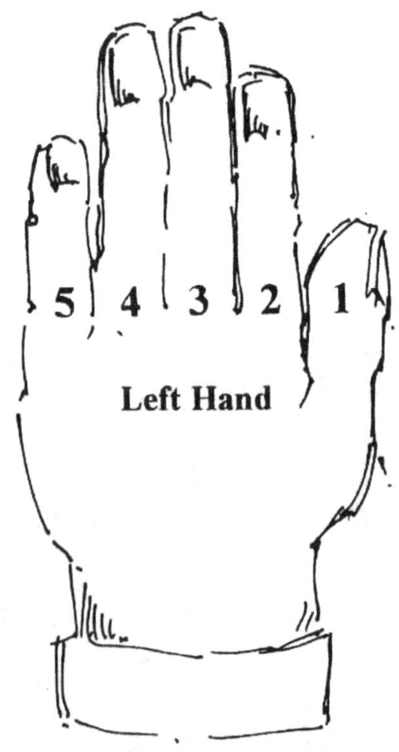

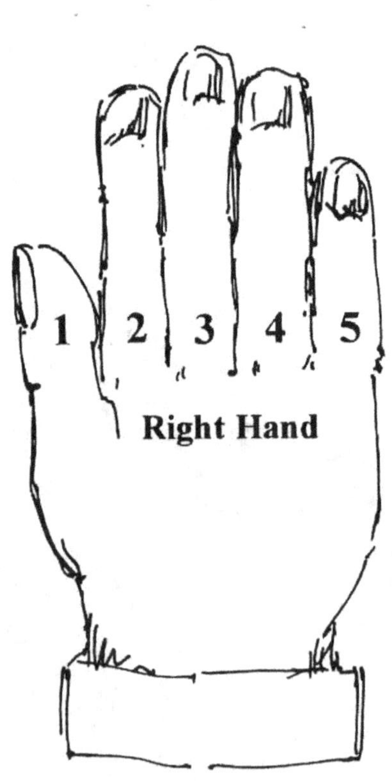

Fig. L The 'C' Chord *(both hands)*

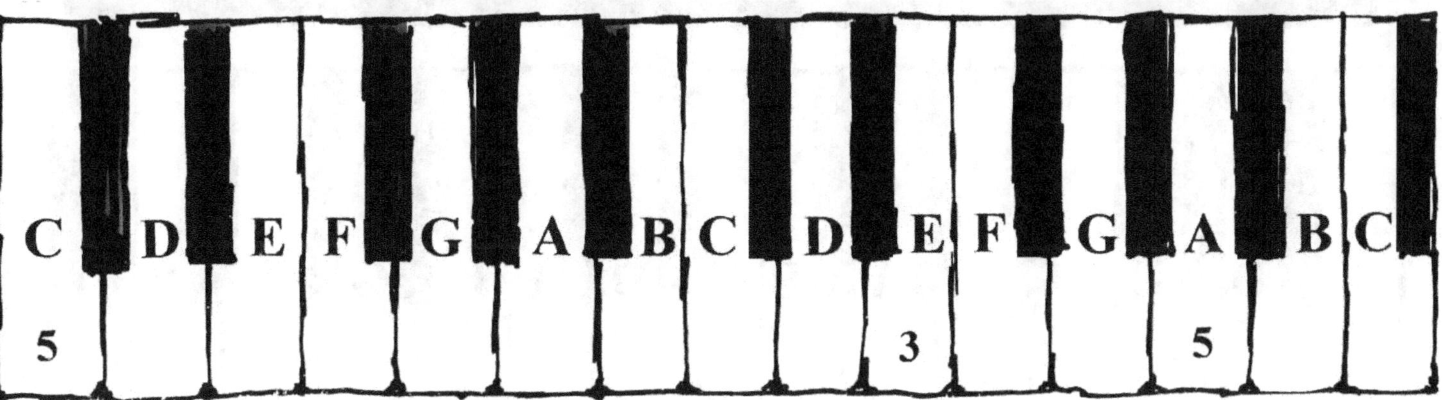

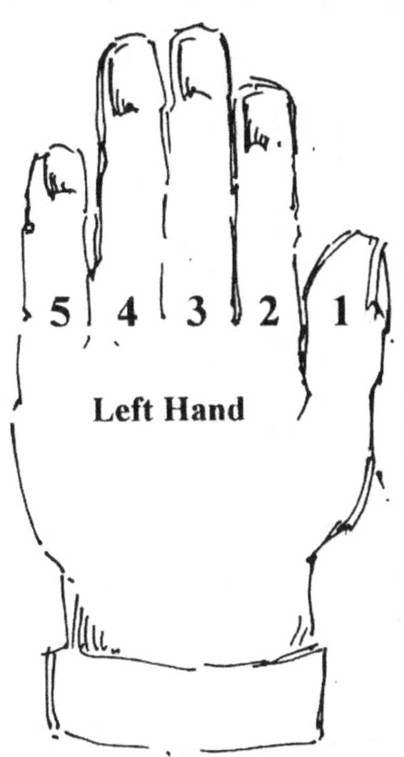

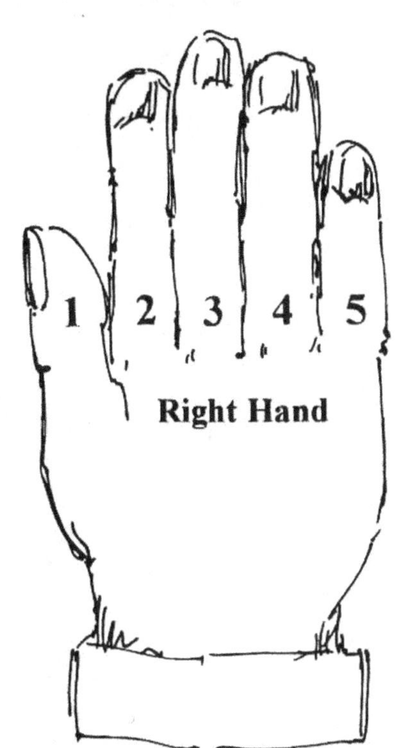

Clementine

$\frac{3}{4}$ c / / | c / / |

c / / | g / / |

g / / | c / / |

g / / | c ‖

Tom Dooley

$\frac{4}{4}$ c / | c g |

g / | g c |

c / | c g |

g / | c / ‖

Fig. M The 'G' Chord *(both Hands)*

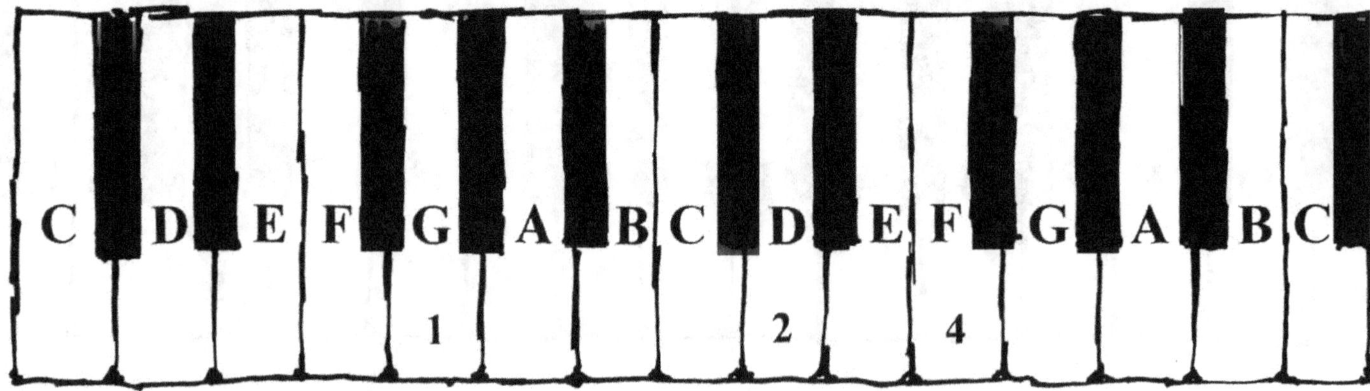

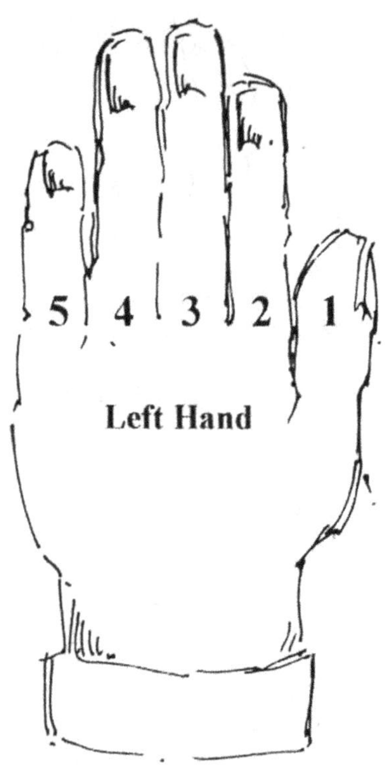

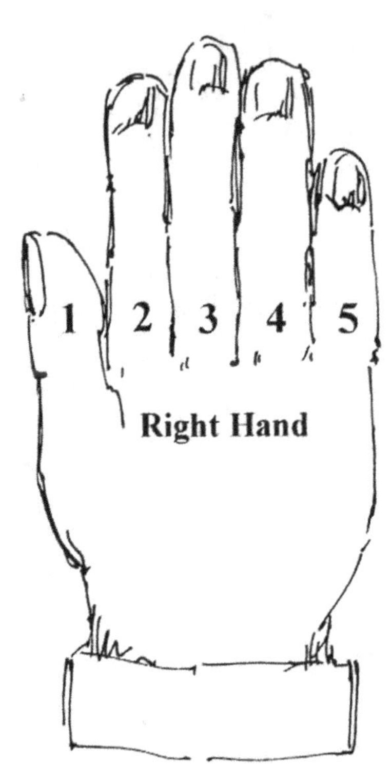

Row, Row, Row Your Boat

$$\frac{4}{4}\ c/\ \ |c/\ \ |$$
$$c/\ \ |g^7\ c\ |$$
$$c/\ \ |c/\ \ |$$
$$c/\ \ |g^7\ c\ \|$$

Mary Had a Little Lamb

$$\frac{4}{4}\ c/\ \ |g^7\ c\ |$$
$$c/\ \ |g^7\ c\ |$$
$$c/\ \ |g^7\ c\ |$$
$$c/\ \ |g^7\ c\ \|$$

Fig. N The 'F' Chord *(both Hands)*

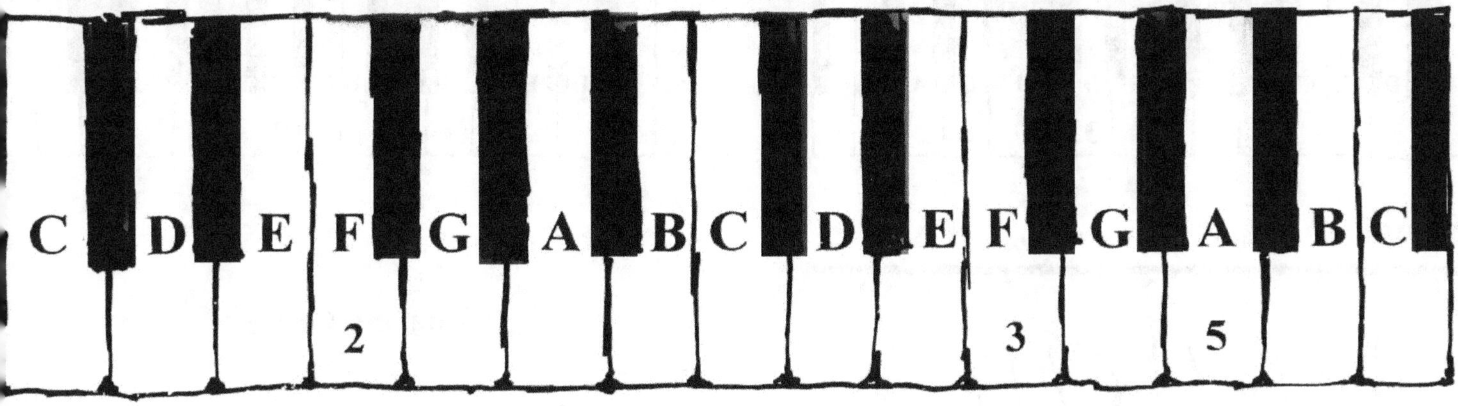

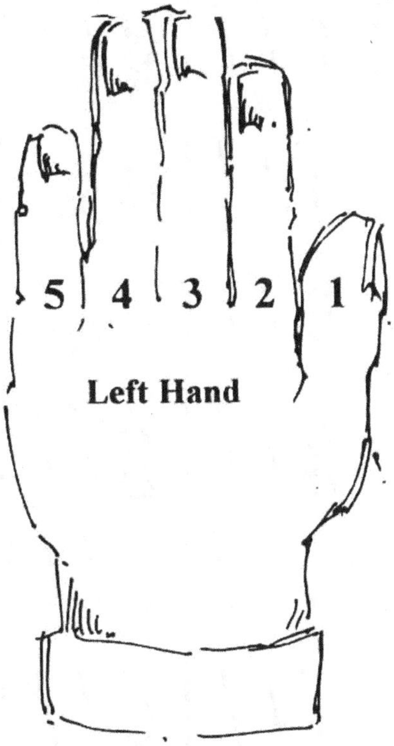

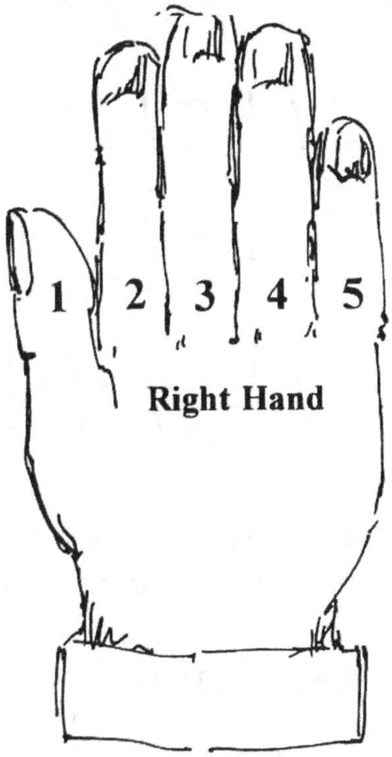

Auld Lang Syne

$\frac{4}{4}$ c / / / | g / / / |

c / / / | f / / / |

c / / / | g / / / |

c / g / | c / / ||

When the Saints Come Marching In

$\frac{4}{4}$ c / / / | c / / / |

c / / / | g / / / |

c / / / | f / / / |

c / g / | c h / / ||

Songs to Play

$$\frac{4}{4}\ c\ /\ /\ /\ |\ c\ /\ /\ /\ |$$

$$f\ /\ c\ /\ |\ g^7\ /\ /\ /\ |$$

$$c\ /\ /\ /\ |\ c\ /\ /\ /\ |$$

$$f\ /\ c\ /\ |\ g^7\ c\ /\ /\ \|\|$$

"Trick" - Alternate the left and right hands to help you prepare for the next change.

Deck the Halls

$$\frac{4}{4}\ c\ /\ /\ /\ |\ g^7 c\ g^7 c\ |$$

$$c\ /\ /\ /\ |\ g^7 c\ g^7 c\ |$$

$$g^7\ c\ /\ /\ |\ c\ /\ g^7\ |$$

$$c\ /\ /\ /\ |\ f\ c\ g^7 c\ \|\|$$

Amazing Grace

$$\frac{3}{4}\ c\ /\ /\ |\ c\ /\ /\ |$$

$$f\ /\ /\ |\ c\ /\ /\ |$$

$$c\ /\ /\ |\ c\ /\ /\ |$$

$$g^7\ /\ /\ |\ g^7\ /\ /\ |$$

$$c\ /\ /\ |\ c\ /\ /\ |$$

$$f\ /\ /\ |\ c\ /\ /\ |$$

$$c\ /\ /\ |\ g^7\ /\ /\ |$$

$$c\ /\ /\ |\ c\ \ \|\|$$

Play the left hand first, then the right hand twice

'F' Chord

Songs to Play

Michael Row Your Boat Ashore

$$\frac{4}{4}\ c\ /\ /\ /\ |\ f\ /\ c\ /\ |$$

$$c\ /\ g^7\ |\ g^7\ c\ \|$$

Also try it with a different rhythm: left hand, then right hand twice as fast, then left hand, then right hand.

She'll be Coming 'Round the Mountain

$$\frac{4}{4}\ c\ /\ /\ /\ |\ c\ /\ /\ /\ |$$

$$c\ /\ /\ /\ |\ g^7\ /\ /\ /\ |$$

$$c\ /\ /\ /\ |\ f\ /\ /\ /\ |$$

$$c\ /\ g^7\ |\ c\ /\ /\ \|$$

Review and practice the 'C', 'G' and 'F' Cords, and you'll be on your way to being able to play many other songs!

This is your last song.

Davey and I practice together and it helps to study with a friend as long as you stay focused.

Here is an brief glossary of some terms and symbols that are used in the book. Try to practice at least a half an hour a day. Don't neglect your other school studies.

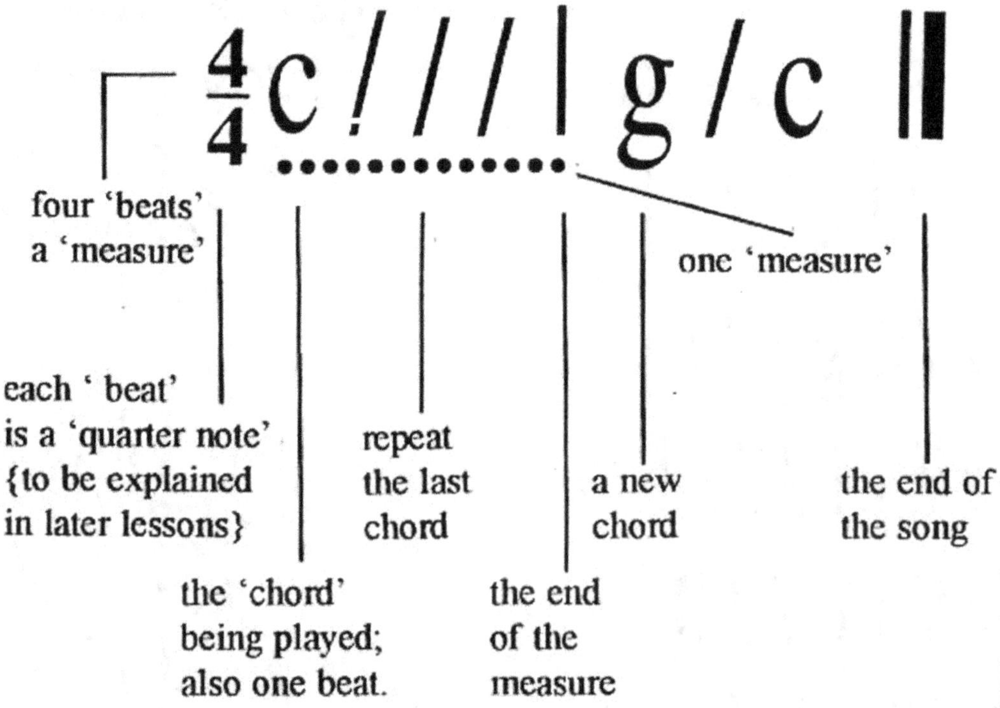

$\frac{4}{4}$ c / / / | g / c ‖

four 'beats'
a 'measure'

one 'measure'

each ' beat'
is a 'quarter note'
{to be explained
in later lessons}

repeat
the last
chord

a new
chord

the end of
the song

the 'chord'
being played;
also one beat.

the end
of the
measure

Keyboards are used in school when you learn theory. Pianos do not need tuning at each use or performance like guitars, bass and other stringed instruments. If you have a grand piano or upright it will take a professional piano tuner to tune your piano. This usually happens after a few years of use. Electric pianos are used by most professionals because they are easier to transport. You can look at music stores or maybe find a used piano on line. If you plan to play in a musical group you will need an electric keyboard. Some keyboards have multiple sounds besides piano. They may have many differnet string instruments and even percussion. The piano is considered both a percussion instrument and a string instrument. Hope this gives you a little understanding about the instrument you are about to learn.

Hope you enjoyed the book!
The gang is coming over to play music today. Tell your friends about us and our other books. Then you will have someone to play music with. Playing music with your friends is so much fun. Remember to practice!

Notes

KIDS BOOKS 1-4 NEW EDOTION
hppt://rockzion.com/marcosharmonicas.html